Level 1	Par

STUDENT ACTIVITIES MANUAL
作业簿
for

Chinese Link
中文天地
Zhōng Wén Tiān Dì

Beginning Chinese

Second Edition

Simplified Character Version

吴素美 Sue-mei Wu
于月明 Yueming Yu
张燕辉 Yanhui Zhang
田维忠 Weizhong Tian

Prentice Hall
Boston Columbus Indianapolis New York San Francisco Upper Saddle River
Amsterdam Cape Town Dubai London Madrid Milan Munich Paris Montréal Toronto
Delhi Mexico City São Paulo Sydney Hong Kong Seoul Singapore Taipei Tokyo

Senior Acquisitions Editor: Rachel McCoy
Editorial Assistant: Noha Amer
Publishing Coordinator: Kathryn Corasaniti
Executive Marketing Manager: Kris Ellis-Levy
Senior Marketing Manager: Denise Miller
Marketing Coordinator: William J. Bliss
Senior Media Editor: Samantha Alducin
Development Editor: Christina Shafermeyer
Development Editor for Assessment: Melissa Marolla Brown
Media Editor: Meriel Martinez
Senior Managing Editor: Mary Rottino
Associate Managing Editor: Janice Stangel
Senior Production Project Manager: Manuel Echevarria
Senior Manufacturing and Operations Manager, Arts and Sciences: Nick Sklitsis
Operations Specialist: Cathleen Petersen
Senior Art Director: Pat Smythe
Art Director: Miguel Ortiz
Cover Image: Jochen Helle
Full-Service Project Management: Margaret Chan, Graphicraft Limited
Printer/Binder: LSC Communications
Cover Printer: LSC Communications
Publisher: Phil Miller

This book was set in 12/15 Sabon by Graphicraft Ltd., Hong Kong.

Printed in the United States of America

Prentice Hall
is an imprint of

PEARSON

www.pearsonhighered.com

ISBN 10: 0-205-74123-1
ISBN 13: 978-0-205-74123-6

21 2022

目录 CONTENTS

前言 PREFACE

The second edition of the ***Student Activities Manual*** for the ***Chinese Link*** contains homework assignments for each lesson in the main textbook. Homework activities are divided among listening exercises, character exercises, grammar exercises, and comprehensive exercises.

Thanks to the many instructors and students who provided valuable feedback on the first edition, the second edition incorporates several new features that we believe will make the materials more effective and easier to use. These new features are highlighted below:

1. For more efficiency and convenience, the ***Workbook*** is now divided into two separate volumes, the ***Student Activities Manual*** and ***Character Book***.

   The new edition of the ***Student Activities Manual*** now provides a greater variety of exercises to consolidate what students have learned for each lesson. It incorporates listening, character, grammar and comprehensive exercises into each lesson's homework.

   The ***Character Book*** now combines both the traditional and simplified character versions.

2. More **challenging and authentic materials** have been added to the listening exercises. Situational dialogues have been created for each lesson that incorporate its themes, expressions, and its pragmatic settings of the lesson. Dialogues also contain some vocabulary and expressions that the students have not yet studied in the hope that these situational dialogues can challenge them from the very beginning and help them develop the skill of picking out useful information even if they don't fully understand everything they hear. This helps develop an important survival skill for students who will encounter real-life settings in Chinese society through study abroad, travel, or interaction with Chinese communities in their own countries.

3. At the end of each lesson's exercises, a **Progress Checklist** is included so that instructors and students can check that the students have accomplished the goals of the lesson and acquired the competencies that the lesson was designed to help them learn.

Sue-mei Wu 吴素美, Ph.D.
Lead author of *Chinese Link*
Carnegie Mellon University

Name: ____________________ Date: ______________

Lesson 12 Making Requests
第十二课 请求

I. Listening Exercises

12-1 Listen and choose the correct meaning for each sentence you hear.

1. a. He wants to know whether I want to have dinner at his home.
   b. He wants to know if he can have dinner at my home.
   c. He told me that I should have dinner at his home.

2. a. You should drink more coffee.
   b. You should not drink coffee.
   c. You should drink less coffee.

3. a. Xiao Li wants me to drive him to the library to borrow two English literature books.
   b. Xiao Li doesn't want to drive to the school's library to borrow two English literature books.
   c. Xiao Li wants to drive to the school's library to borrow two English literature books.

4. a. It will take five days to drive from New York[1] to Los Angeles.[2]
   b. It won't take five days to drive from New York to Los Angeles.
   c. We shouldn't drive from New York to Los Angeles.

5. a. I will go home to see my mother in May next year.
   b. I will go home to see my mother in May this year.
   c. I will go home to see my mother in June this year.

6. a. Tomorrow I can use the computer[3] my friend lent me to write an email to Xiao Wang.
   b. Tomorrow I will use the computer Xiao Wang lent me to write an email to my friend.
   c. Tomorrow I cannot use the computer my friend lent me to write an email to Xiao Wang.

Notes: 1. 纽约 [Niǔyuē]: New York
2. 洛杉矶 [Luòshānjī]: Los Angeles
3. 电脑 [diànnǎo]: computer

12-2 Listen to the dialogue between 方明英 and 丁文. Then choose whether the following statements are true or false.

1. 丁文很想看这个中国电影*。	True	False
2. 丁文明天下午没有课。	True	False
3. 每天下午有车从宿舍到中美图书馆。	True	False
4. 丁文要跟方明英一起看电影。	True	False

**Note:* 电影 [diànyǐng]: movie

12-3 Listen to the challenge dialogue. Though there may be some words and phrases that are unfamiliar to you, see if you can understand the general meaning by using what you have learned. Then choose whether the following statements are true or false.

1. 本乐's roommate is coming back from China.	True	False
2. 于影 is going to give a presentation tomorrow morning.	True	False
3. 本乐 will let 于影 borrow his notebook computer.	True	False

12-4 Listen to the challenge dialogue again and choose the best answer for each of the following questions.

1. What is 本乐 doing now?
   a. He is surfing the Internet.
   b. He is having dinner.
   c. He is going to the airport.
   d. He is reading a book.

2. Who is back from Beijing?
   a. 于影 b. 本乐 c. 本乐's girlfriend d. 本乐's roommate

3. When will 本乐 and 于影 meet again?
   a. Tonight at 8:00.
   b. Tomorrow morning.
   c. This afternoon at 5:00.
   d. Tomorrow afternoon at 5:00.

Name: ________________ Date: ____________

II. Character Exercises

12-5 Choose the correct traditional form for each of the following characters.

1. 飞 a. 樂 b. 從 c. 飛
2. 习 a. 書 b. 習 c. 時
3. 开 a. 幾 b. 兒 c. 開
4. 应 a. 應 b. 會 c. 麼
5. 练 a. 給 b. 練 c. 紹
6. 进 a. 還 b. 這 c. 進

12-6 Write the Chinese characters for the following phrases.

1. wǒ děi qù jīchǎng jiē wǒ mèimei ____________________
2. yīnggāi méi wèntí ____________________
3. wǒde Zhōngwén jìnbù le ____________________
4. wǒde chē shì báisè de ____________________
5. tíng zài wǔ hào tíngchē chǎng ____________________

III. Grammar Exercises

12-7 Choose an optative verb from the box to complete the following sentences. Note that more than one answer may be possible in some cases.

要，想，应该，得，能，可以，会

1. 他们 _____ 坐飞机从纽约来这儿玩儿。
2. 我的爸爸妈妈都 _____ 说中文，你 _____ 跟他们说中文。
3. 她 _____ 会开手排挡的车。
4. 我今天晚上 _____ 借你的车吗？

12-8 Use negative optative verbs to turn the following positive sentences into negative sentences.

1. 我要在早上六点起床。

    ____

2. 我们想多喝点茶。

    ____

3. 小美应该多练习开车。

    ____

4. 我能借老师的书。

    ____

5. 在宿舍可以看电视。

    ____

6. 老师今天会晚点儿下课。

    ____

7. 你得开车去机场。

    ____

8. 她应该少喝咖啡，多喝水。

    ____

Name: ____________________ Date: ______________

IV. Comprehensive Exercises

12-9 Read the following passage and then answer the questions below.

我叫李红英，我在华中大学学工程。我的爸爸妈妈都是中国人，可是我在美国出生[1]，也在美国长大[2]。我小的时候，爸爸妈妈说我应该学中文。可是我不喜欢学中文。爸爸妈妈跟我说中文的时候，我总是[3]跟他们说英文。

上大学以后我认识到[4]学中文很重要，于是[5]我非常想学中文了。去年八月的时候，我去问华中大学中文系的王老师我应该上哪个中文班。王老师问我的中文怎么样。我说我能说一点儿中文，可是我一个中文字也不会写。王老师说我应该在一年级[6]学中文。

Notes:

1. 出生 [chūshēng]: born
2. 长大 [zhǎngdà]: grow up
3. 总是 [zǒngshì]: always
4. 认识到 [rènshidào]: realize
5. 于是 [yúshì]: therefore
6. 一年级 [yī niánjí]: 1st year

1. 李红英在哪个大学学习？她学什么？

   ____

2. 李红英小的时候跟爸爸妈妈说中文吗？

   ____

3. 上中文课以前，李红英会说中文、写中文吗？

   ____

4. 王老师说李红英应该上哪个中文班？

   ____

12-10 Answer the following questions in Chinese.

1. 你想不想学二年级的中文?

    ____

2. 你会不会说法文? 日文呢?

    ____

3. 你会不会开手排挡的车?

    ____

4. 你可以不可以晚上十一点以后去图书馆借书?

    ____

Progress Checklist

After this lesson, you should be able to use Chinese to:

( ) borrow something from someone,

( ) tell others what they should or should not do,

( ) ask others what they would like to do,

( ) ask/give permission to do something,

( ) ask/tell about someone's capabilities for doing something (e.g., driving a car, language skills),

( ) express the possibility of something occurring.

Name: ____________ Date: ____________

Lesson 13 Clothes and Shopping
第十三课 衣服、逛街

I. Listening Exercises

13-1 Listen to the dialogue between 方明飞 and 店员. Then choose whether the following statements are true or false.

1. 方明飞想买一件衬衫。 True False
2. 店员给他看看蓝色和黑色的裤子。 True False
3. 方明飞喜欢黑色的裤子。 True False
4. 店员说黄衬衫很好看。 True False
5. 方明飞说黑色的衬衫很不错。 True False

13-2 Listen to the sentences and fill in the blanks with the words you hear.

1. 我想买一 ____ 衬衫 ________ 一条裤子。
2. 你 ________ 看看。我 ____ 这件好吗?
3. 这条裙子 ____________?
4. 请 ____________ 。
5. 我 ________ 喜欢黑色的大衣。

13-3 Listen to the challenge dialogue. Though there may be some words and phrases that are unfamiliar to you, see if you can understand the general meaning by using what you have learned. Then choose whether the following statements are true or false.

1. They are talking about a computer.	True	False
2. 爱红's boyfriend doesn't buy skirts for her.	True	False
3. 爱红 is wearing a green skirt.	True	False

13-4 Listen to the challenge dialogue again and choose the best answer for each of the following questions.

1. Where are 爱红 and 子英 now?
   a. They are in a clothing store.
   b. They are in a restaurant.
   c. They are sitting in front of a computer.
   d. They are in the movie theater.

2. What color of skirt does 爱红 like?
   a. Green.
   b. Red.
   c. White.
   d. Yellow.

3. What would 爱红 like to do now?
   a. She is going to the store to buy another skirt.
   b. She is going to return the clothes she doesn't like.
   c. She is going to try on the skirt she bought.
   d. She is going to look at clothes online with 子英.

Name: ______________ Date: ____________

II. Character Exercises

13-5 Choose the correct traditional form for each of the following characters.

1. 衬　　a. 衫　b. 襯　c. 見
2. 觉　　a. 覺　b. 黃　c. 幫
3. 买　　a. 賣　b. 買　c. 票
4. 裤　　a. 衣　b. 裙　c. 褲
5. 让　　a. 讓　b. 試　c. 說

13-6 Match the Pinyin with the corresponding Chinese character.

_____	1. wèi	a. 穿
_____	2. chuān	b. 裙
_____	3. tiáo	c. 试
_____	4. mǎi	d. 位
_____	5. qún	e. 条
_____	6. ràng	f. 衫
_____	7. shì	g. 买
_____	8. shān	h. 让

III. Grammar Exercises

13-7 Write the correct measure words.

1. 一 ____ 裤子
2. 两 ____ 衬衫
3. 三 ____ 鞋
4. 四 ____ 裙子
5. 五 ____ 牛仔裤
6. 六 ____ 运动衫
7. 七 ____ 小狗
8. 八 ____ 电影票

13-8 Answer the questions below using 或者.

1. 你回家以后想做什么?

____

2. 这张电影票是谁的?

____

3. 我们去哪个餐馆吃饭?

____

4. 你喜欢黄衬衫吗?

____

Name: ____________________ Date: ______________

IV. Comprehensive Exercises

13-9 Complete the following dialogues, using the clues given in parentheses.

1. **A:** 你说那件衬衫怎么样?

   B: ______________________________。(Let me have a look.)

2. **A:** 我应该穿几号的?

   B: ______________________________。(Try a size 6 or a size 7.)

3. **A:** 我不知道这个电影是说什么的。

   B: ______________________________。(I'll give you a little introduction.)

4. **A:** 上海春卷真好吃。

   B: 真的吗? ______________________________。(I'll taste it as well.)

5. **A:** 手排挡的车我还不会开。

   B: ______________________________。(You should learn how to drive.)

13-10 Describe a recent shopping trip. (Use approximately 80–100 characters.)

____

____

____

____

____

____

____

____

Progress Checklist

After this lesson, you should be able to use Chinese to:

( ) name different types of clothing,

( ) express what you would like to buy,

( ) express what color(s) you like,

( ) provide your opinions of clothing (e.g., looks good/bad, expensive/cheap, etc.),

( ) ask/tell how much something costs.

Name: ____________________ Date: ______________

Lesson 14 Birthdays and Celebrations
第十四课 生日和庆祝

I. Listening Exercises

14-1 Listen to the sentences and fill in the blanks with the words you hear.

1. 三月十八日是我的 ______________ 。

2. 我今年 ______________ ，______________ 二十岁。

3. ______________ 是我的生日 ______________ 。请你 ______________ 。

14-2 Listen to the dialogue. Then choose the best answer for each of the following questions.

1. How old is Xingxing?
   a. She is twenty.
   b. She is twenty-one.
   c. She is twenty-two.
   d. She is twenty-three.

2. When is Mingming's birthday party?
   a. This Friday. b. Next Friday. c. This Saturday. d. Next Saturday.

3. How old is Mingming going to be?
   a. Twenty. b. Twenty-one. c. Twenty-two. d. Twenty-three.

4. Who does Mingming say will also be coming to his birthday party?
   a. Lots of his friends.
   b. His father and his girlfriend.
   c. His classmates and his brother.
   d. His sister and his sister's boyfriend.

5. Who will make the birthday cake?
   a. His roommate. b. His friend. c. Xingxing. d. His mom.

14-3 Listen to the challenge dialogue. Though there may be some words and phrases that are unfamiliar to you, see if you can understand the general meaning by using what you have learned. Then choose whether the following statements are true or false.

1. They are talking about last year's Chinese New Year party. True False
2. 爱红 is going to 子英's party tonight. True False
3. 子英 is going to learn how to make a birthday cake and a Chinese New Year cake. True False

14-4 Listen to the challenge dialogue again and choose the best answer for each of the following questions.

1. What does 爱红 give 子英 as a birthday present?
   a. A new book
   b. A birthday cake.
   c. Dumplings.
   d. A pack of tea.
2. How does 爱红 know about 子英's birthday?
   a. She heard it from 子英's roommate.
   b. She is 子英's roommate.
   c. 子英 told her in the past.
   d. She heard it from 子英's boyfriend.
3. When is 爱红's birthday?
   a. On the 10th of last month.
   b. On the 10th of next month.
   c. Today.
   d. During the Christmas holiday.

Name: ________________ Date: ____________

II. Character Exercises

14-5 Match each traditional character with its simplified form.

_____ 1. 歲 a. 会

_____ 2. 過 b. 为

_____ 3. 為 c. 图

_____ 4. 參 d. 气

_____ 5. 氣 e. 参

_____ 6. 會 f. 岁

_____ 7. 圖 g. 过

14-6 Write the following Pinyin sentences in Chinese characters.

1. Wǒde shēngrì shì yīyuè sān shí hào, xīngqīsì.

____

2. Zhè shì nǐde péngyou sòng nǐde dà dàngāo ma?

____

3. Nǐ jīnnián duō dà? Wǒ jīnnián shíjiǔ suì.

____

III. Grammar Exercises

14-7 Fill in the blanks according to this year's calendar.

1. 今年春节 [Chūnjié] (Spring Festival / Chinese New Year) 是 ________________ (date), ________________ (day of the week) 。

2. 今天是 ________________ (date), ________________ (day of the week) 。

3. 下个星期日是 ________________ (date) 。

4. 今年的感恩节 [Gǎn'ēnjié] (Thanksgiving) 是 ________________ (date) ________________ (day of the week) 。

5. 圣诞节 [Shèngdànjié] (Christmas) 是 ________________ (date) ________________ (day of the week) 。

6. 我的生日是 ________________ (date), 今年在 ________________ (day of the week) 。

14-8 Rewrite the following sentences to include 为 and another person.

1. 我要做蛋糕。

____

2. 我妈妈想买衬衫。

____

3. 小明要去图书馆借中文书。

____

4. 妹妹要做炒面。

____

5. 我们想开中文班的晚会。

____

Name: ____________ Date: ____________

IV. Comprehensive Exercises

14-9 Complete the following sentences, using the clues given in parentheses.

1. 下个星期日我要 ______________________________ 。
(hold a birthday party for my friend)

2. 你可以 ______________________________ ?
(make an order of Chinese dumplings for me)

3. 后天是妈妈的生日，我要 ______________________________ 。
(buy a very pretty shirt for her)

14-10 You've called a friend to invite them to your roommate's birthday party next Saturday. Your friend wasn't home so you left a message. Write down what you said in your message. Try to include the following words and expressions (as well as other words and expressions you have learned).

生日　空　晚会　月　号　还是　为　参加　知道　地址

____

____

____

____

____

____

____

____

Progress Checklist

After this lesson, you should be able to use Chinese to:

( ) ask/tell dates and days of the week,

( ) ask someone when their birthday is and how old they are,

( ) tell someone when your birthday is and how old you are,

( ) invite someone to a birthday party.

Name: ____________ Date: ____________

Lesson 15 Location and Position
第十五课 地点和位置

I. Listening Exercises

15-1 Listen to Liang Zhi's introduction of his dorm. Draw a floor plan based on what you hear.

15-2 Choose whether each statement below is true or false according to Liang Zhi's introduction.

1. His dorm is on the third floor. True False
2. His dorm doesn't have a kitchen. True False
3. His dorm is spacious. True False
4. The library is next to his dorm. True False
5. He likes to read in his dorm. True False

15-3 Listen to the challenge dialogue. Though there may be some words and phrases that are unfamiliar to you, see if you can understand the general meaning by using what you have learned. Then choose whether the following statements are true or false.

1. Bao Zhizhong's dorm is small. True False
2. Bao Zhizhong's dorm has two bedrooms. True False
3. There is a kitchen in the dorm. True False

15-4 Listen to the challenge dialogue again and choose the best answer for each of the following questions.

1. Where is Bao Zhizhong's dorm?
   a. By the shopping center.
   b. Behind the library.
   c. Next to Tian Jin's apartment.
   d. Next to a cafe.
2. It takes ten minutes to walk from which place to Bao Zhizhong's dorm?
   a. From the cafe.
   b. From the library.
   c. From Tiao Jin's apartment.
   d. From school.
3. Where do Bao Zhizhong and his roommate usually go to study?
   a. Bao Zhizhong studies in the library, while his roommate studies in the dorm.
   b. They both study in the library.
   c. Bao Zhizhong studies in the dorm, while his roommate studies in the library.
   d. They both study in the dorm.

Name: ________________ Date: ______________

II. Character Exercises

15-5 Write the letter of the correct position word for each question.

a. 里边　　b. 旁边　　c. 对面　　d. 上边　　e. 中间　　f. 后边

1.  中文书在桌子的什么地方？ ____

2.  小明在他朋友的什么地方？ ____

3.  小明在文中的什么地方？ ____

4. 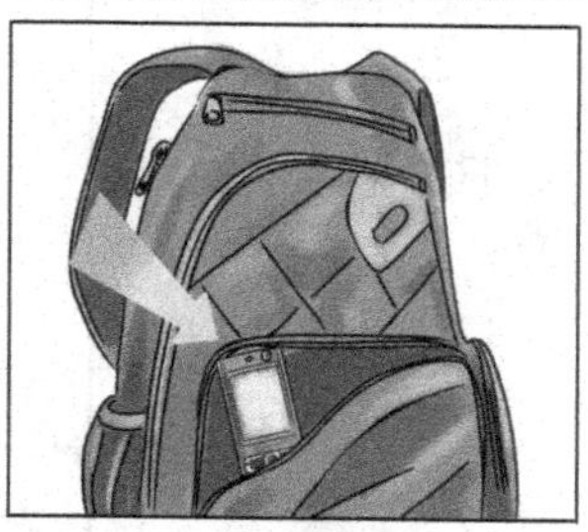 手机在背包的哪儿？ ____

5.  中文老师在桌子的什么地方？ ____

6. 

图书馆在宿舍的什么地方？ ____

15-6 Match the Chinese characters with the corresponding Pinyin.

_____	1. 卧室	a. chúfáng
_____	2. 客厅	b. wòshì
_____	3. 厨房	c. cāntīng
_____	4. 公园	d. cānguān
_____	5. 餐厅	e. gōngyòng
_____	6. 洗澡	f. kètīng
_____	7. 参观	g. xǐzǎo
_____	8. 公用	h. gōngyuán

III. Grammar Exercises

15-7 Look at the following floor plan for an apartment in the new dorm. Then answer the questions that follow.

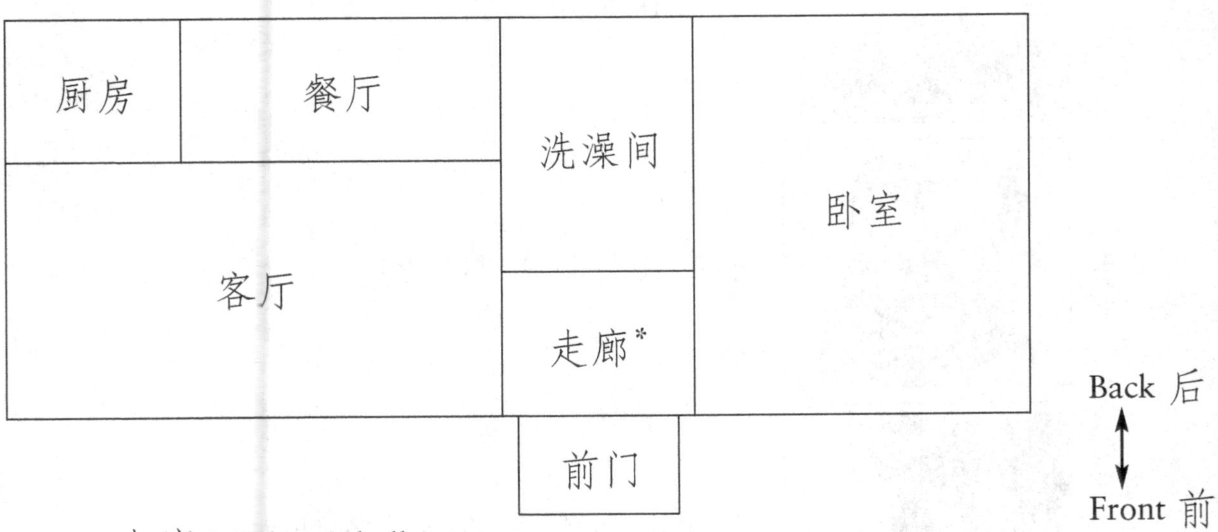

**Note:* 走廊 [zǒuláng]: hallway

1. 卧室在哪儿?

____

2. 卧室的对面是什么?

____

Name: ______________ Date: ____________

3. 厨房和洗澡间的中间是什么？

____

4. 客厅和卧室的中间有什么？

____

5. 餐厅在客厅的哪边？

____

15-8 Look at the pictures and fill in the blanks with 有, 在, 是.

1.

裙子 ____ 鞋子的右边[1]。

裙子的左边[2] ____ 鞋子。

2.

房子的后边 ____ 一棵[3]树[4]。

房子 ____ 树的前边。

3.

球的左边 ____ 一件衬衫，鞋子 ____ 球的下边。

衬衫 ____ 球的左边，球的下边 ____ 鞋子。

Notes: 1. 右边 [yòubiān]: right
2. 左边 [zuǒbiān]: left
3. 棵 [kē]: measure word for plants
4. 树 [shù]: tree

IV. Comprehensive Exercises

15-9 You work part-time at a real-estate office. Part of your job is to write introductions of houses for brochures. Write an introduction for a house in which you describe the rooms and the house's location. The following words and expressions can be used, as well other words and expressions that you have learned.

大门	[dàmén]	main gate	楼梯	[lóutī]	stairs
车库	[chēkù]	garage	院子	[yuànzi]	(court)yard
地下室	[dìxiàshì]	basement			

____

____

____

____

____

Progress Checklist

After this lesson, you should be able to use Chinese to:

( ) use position words to specify the relative location of something (e.g., front/back; top/under; inside/outside; left/right; beside, middle and opposite),

( ) use 在, 有, and 是 to ask/tell the location or existence of something,

( ) show people around (e.g., give a tour of your home or school).

Name: ____________________ Date: ______________

Lesson 16 Hobbies and Sports
第十六课 爱好和运动

I. Listening Exercises

16-1 Listen to the dialogue. Then choose the best answer for each of the following questions.

1. Where is she going?
   a. She is going to a class.
   b. She is going to play basketball.
   c. She is going back to her dorm to make dumplings.

2. How well does he play basketball?
   a. He plays very well.
   b. He doesn't play very well.
   c. He often practices and is improving.

3. Does she like to swim?
   a. She likes to swim, and swims quite well.
   b. She likes to swim, but doesn't swim very well.
   c. She doesn't like to swim.

4. What's their plan for tonight?
   a. They will go to swim together.
   b. They will go to basketball together.
   c. They will have dumplings at her dorm.

16-2 Listen and choose the statement that is correct.

1. a. 小美做饭做得很慢。
   b. 小美吃饭吃得很慢。

2. a. 欢欢篮球打得不太好。
   b. 欢欢篮球打得很好。

3. a. 正然作业做得很好。
   b. 正然写字写得很快。

16-3 Listen to the challenge dialogue. Though there may be some words and phrases that are unfamiliar to you, see if you can understand the general meaning by using what you have learned. Then choose whether the following statements are true or false.

1. 张正然 and 孙信美 don't know how to play basketball. True False
2. 杨欢 can run very fast. True False
3. Today is Friday. True False

16-4 Listen to the challenge dialogue again and choose the best answer for each of the following questions.

1. What are the three friends going to do at 5:00?
   a. Dine in a restaurant.
   b. Watch a movie.
   c. Play basketball in the stadium.
   d. Walk to the dorm.
2. How does 杨欢 go to meet 张正然 and 孙信美?
   a. She drives.
   b. She takes a bus.
   c. She runs.
   d. She rides a bike.
4. Why is 杨欢 almost late?
   a. She went swimming before coming.
   b. Her Literature class ended later than usual.
   c. She went to play basketball before coming.
   d. She had Chinese food before coming.

Name: ________________ Date: ____________

II. Character Exercises

16-5 Match each traditional character with its simplified form.

____ 1. 鍛　　a. 篮

____ 2. 籃　　b. 体

____ 3. 體　　c. 边

____ 4. 圖　　d. 厅

____ 5. 邊　　e. 图

____ 6. 業　　f. 锻

____ 7. 廳　　g. 业

16-6 Write the following Pinyin sentences in Chinese characters.

1. Tā jiāode hěnhǎo.

____

2. Wǒ yóuyǒng yóu de hěnkuài.

____

3. Nǐ xiànzài yàobuyào gēn wǒmen qù duànliàn?

____

4. Lánqiú wǒ hái dǎde bú tài hǎo.

____

III. Grammar Exercises

16-7 Write the following sentences in Chinese, using 得 to describe actions.

1. He came very early.

____

2. I often eat very slowly.

____

3. You walk too fast.

____

4. He plays basketball very well.

____

5. My roommate goes to bed very late.

____

6. My mom makes dumplings very fast.

____

16-8 Rewrite the following sentences so that emphasis is placed on the object of each sentence.

1. 她打篮球打得不错。

____

2. 妈妈包饺子包得非常快。

____

3. 谁做饭做得很好?

____

4. 我睡觉睡得太少。

____

Name: ______________ Date: ____________

IV. Comprehensive Exercises

16-9 Read the following passage and then answer the questions below.

包健和杨中是室友。他们俩都非常喜欢运动，常常一起去健身房锻炼。包健游泳游得很好，他是学校游泳队[1]的，他也是杨中的游泳教练。杨中游得也不错，可是他不常常游泳。

包健喜欢打篮球，他打得非常好。他也喜欢打排球[2]和乒乓球[3]。排球和乒乓球他都打得不错。

他们俩也喜欢做饭。包健包饺子包得很快，也很好看。杨中做中国菜做得很好吃。他们也常常请同学们去他们的宿舍吃饭。

Notes:
1. 队 [duì]: team
2. 排球 [páiqiú]: volleyball
3. 乒乓球 [pīngpāngqiú]: table tennis

1. 包健和杨中常常去哪儿?

____

2. 包健喜欢打什么球? 他打得怎么样?

____

3. 杨中常游泳吗? 他游得怎么样?

____

4. 他们俩做饭做得怎么样?

____

5. 同学们常常去他们宿舍做什么?

____

16-10 Write a short dialogue between 包健 and 杨中 based on the above reading in Activity 16-9.

____

____

____

____

____

____

Progress Checklist

After this lesson, you should be able to use Chinese to:

( ) ask someone what sports they like,

( ) tell others which sports you like,

( ) ask someone how well they do a certain sport or activity,

( ) tell others how well you do certain sports or activities,

( ) talk about where, with whom, and how often you or others do a certain sport or activity.

Name: ____________ Date: ____________

Lesson 17 Weather and Seasons
第十七课 天气和四季

I. Listening Exercises

17-1 Listen and choose the sentence that best describes the statement you hear.

1. a. Spring is coming soon, and the weather is getting warm.
   b. Winter is coming soon, and the weather is getting cold.
   c. Summer is coming soon, and the weather is getting hot.

2. a. She likes spring the most.
   b. She likes summer the most.
   c. She likes fall the most.

3. a. It is not so hot in summer here.
   b. It is very hot in summer here.
   c. It rains a lot in summer here.

4. a. It has been cold the past couple of days.
   b. It rained a lot this week.
   c. It has been extremely hot the past couple of days.

5. a. I'll go to your place during spring break.
   b. Why don't you come over during spring break?
   c. Let's go back home together during summer.

17-2 Listen to the dialogue between 夏华 and 春红. Then choose whether the following statements are true or false.

1. 春红这个学期不忙。	True	False
2. 春红就要参加学校的篮球赛了。	True	False
3. 夏华在春假的时候要回家。	True	False
4. 夏华就要和她的好朋友见面了。	True	False

17-3 Listen to the challenge dialogue. Though there may be some words and phrases that are unfamiliar to you, see if you can understand the general meaning by using what you have learned. Then choose whether the following statements are true or false.

1. It's warm today.	True	False
2. Xiaoling doesn't have a winter coat.	True	False
3. Dazhong suggests that Xiaoling can swim during her vacation.	True	False

17-4 Listen to the challenge dialogue again and choose the best answer for each of the following questions.

1. Where is Dazhong going in the winter break?
   a. To Hawaii.
   b. To China.
   c. To go shopping.
   d. To New York.

2. When is Xiaoling going to travel with her parents?
   a. The weekend.
   b. Winter vacation.
   c. Summer.
   d. Spring.

3. Where is Dazhong's sister living?
   a. China.
   b. Hawaii.
   c. New York.
   d. In this city.

Name: ____________ Date: __________

II. Character Exercises

17-5 Write the Chinese characters for the following English sentences and phrases.

1. Autumn is very warm. ____________________
2. Spring break ____________________
3. It is rainy sometimes in winter. ____________________
4. 100 Fahrenheit ____________________
5. extremely hot ____________________
6. Time flies. ____________________

17-6 Match the Pinyin with the corresponding Chinese characters.

_____	1. qìhòu	a. 冬天
_____	2. dōngtiān	b. 华氏
_____	3. fàngjià	c. 放假
_____	4. xiàyǔ	d. 气候
_____	5. huáshì	e. 好久
_____	6. nuǎnhuo	f. 下雨
_____	7. shíjiān	g. 刮风
_____	8. hǎojiǔ	h. 暖和
_____	9. guāfēng	i. 见面
_____	10. jiànmiàn	j. 时间

III. Grammar Exercises

17-7 Rewrite the following sentences to include a pattern from the box.

……的时候	就要/快要……了	其中

1. 我有一辆白色的车。

   ____

2. 她的弟弟今年十八岁。

   ____

3. 这个学期我有五门课。我最喜欢中文课。

   ____

4. 开车不应该打手机。

   ____

17-8 Unscramble the following sentences by placing the characters in the correct order.

1. 下雪/这儿的/冷/，/常常/冬天/非常

   ____

2. 一百度/，/极了/会到/华氏/夏天/热

   ____

3. 气候/都有/这儿的/春夏秋冬/，/夏天/喜欢/我/最/其中

   ____

4. 就要/了/来/春天/，/放春假/我们/了/也/快要

   ____

Name: ________________ Date: ____________

IV. Comprehensive Exercises

17-9 Answer the following questions in Chinese.

1. 你现在怎么样? 忙不忙?

___

2. 春夏秋冬，其中你最喜欢哪一个?

___

3. 这儿的夏天热不热?

___

4. 这儿的冬天常下雪吗?

___

5. 你们就要放春假了，是吗?

___

6. 春假的时候，你想做什么?

___

17-10 Write a paragraph describing the climate of the place where you come from. Try to include the following words and phrases in your paragraph. (Use at least 100 characters.)

……的时候，就要/快要……了，其中，最，极了，华氏/摄氏

___

___

___

___

___

___

Progress Checklist

After this lesson, you should be able to use Chinese to:

( ) talk about the weather and seasons,

( ) talk about the temperature,

( ) talk about which season you like/dislike the most,

( ) express that something is going to happen in the near future,

( ) write a letter.

Name: ____________________ Date: ______________

Lesson 18 Travel and Transportation
第十八课 旅行和交通

I. Listening Exercises

18-1 Listen to the dialogue. Then choose the best answer for each of the following questions.

1. What will he do during spring break?
   a. He will stay here.
   b. He will go back home.
   c. He will visit a friend.
   d. He will go to the South.

2. Who will he spend the spring break with?
   a. His family.
   b. His friend who lives in New York.
   c. His friend who lives in Canada.
   d. His sister.

3. What means of transportation will he use?
   a. He will drive his brother's car.
   b. He will take an airplane and train.
   c. He will take a train and rent a car.
   d. He will take an airplane and rent a car.

4. Where will she go during spring break?
   a. She will stay here.
   b. She will go home.
   c. She will visit her sister in the South.
   d. She will visit her sister in Canada.

5. Where did he recommend that she go?
   a. To New York.
   b. To the beach.
   c. To a swimming pool.
   d. To Canada.

18-2 Listen to the questions and then give answers based on your own situation.

1. ______________________________

2. ______________________________

3. ______________________________

4. ______________________________

5. ______________________________

18-3 Listen to the challenge dialogue. Though there may be some words and phrases that are unfamiliar to you, see if you can understand the general meaning by using what you have learned. Then choose whether the following statements are true or false.

1. It usually takes him an hour to get to school by bike.	True	False
2. He thinks it is good exercise riding his bike to school.	True	False
3. She will go to Shanghai to visit friends during spring break.	True	False

18-4 Listen to the challenge dialogue again and choose the best answer for each of the following questions.

1. How often does she take the bus to school?
   - a. Every day.
   - b. Never.
   - c. Three days a week.
   - d. Every Monday.

2. Why did he take the bus to school today?
   - a. His car is not working.
   - b. His bike is broken.
   - c. His friend borrowed his bike.
   - d. It is snowing today.

3. How does he go to school on snowy days?
   - a. By bike.
   - b. He walks.
   - c. He borrows his friend's car.
   - d. By bus.

Name: ____________________ Date: ______________

II. Character Exercises

18-5 Write the following Pinyin sentences in Chinese characters.

1. Wǒ jiā lí xuéxiào bù yuǎn, zǒulù zhǐyào shí fēnzhōng.

____

2. Tā yǒushíhou zuò gōnggòng qìchē lái xuéxiào.

____

3. Wǒ cháng qí zìxíngchē, kěyǐ duànlian duànlian.

____

4. Nǐmen zěnme qù lǚxíng? Zuò huǒchē, zuò chuán, kāichē, háishì zuò fēijī?

____

18-6 Match each traditional character with its simplified form.

_____	1. 離	a. 骑
_____	2. 車	b. 离
_____	3. 騎	c. 听
_____	4. 風	d. 钟
_____	5. 聽	e. 车
_____	6. 邊	f. 风
_____	7. 鐘	g. 边

III. Grammar Exercises

18-7 The following are things 文健 is going to do on different days this week. Decide what order 文健 will do each activity and write a sentence using 先, 再, and 然后 to describe the order of events.

1. 星期一：吃早饭　上课　游泳

____

2. 星期二：去图书馆　做功课

____

3. 星期四：看朋友　打电话给朋友

____

4. 星期五：上网　去图书馆　去买东西*

____

**Note:* 东西 [dōngxi]: things

18-8 Complete the following sentences with a verb phrase based on the artwork clues.

1. 从美国去中国，你得 ______________ 。

2. 春假她要 __________ 回家看爸爸妈妈。

Name: ____________ Date: ____________

3. A: 我们怎么去这个饭馆？

   B: 我们坐 ____________ 去。

4. A: 你会 ____________ 吗？

   B: 不会。我会 ____________。

IV. Comprehensive Exercises

18-9 Translate the following sentences into Chinese.

1. Does your younger sister live off campus? Is it far from her school?

   ____

2. I usually ride a bike to campus. When it's raining or snowing, I'll walk.

   ____

3. We want to travel to the West by train. We can look at the scenery on the way.

   ____

4. I've heard that the shore is beautiful in the South. I would like to go there to swim.

   ____

18-10 You are chatting with your roommate about your plans for the coming summer. Write a paragraph about your plans beginning with the following sentence. Be sure to include where you are going, what you are going to do, and what transportation you will use.

我们就要放暑假了……

____

____

____

____

____

____

____

____

Progress Checklist

After this lesson, you should be able to use Chinese to:

( ) ask someone if they live near or far from school, or another location,

( ) ask someone about their daily means of transportation,

( ) tell others how near or far something is,

( ) describe your daily means of transportation,

( ) describe how long it takes to go somewhere by different means of transportation,

( ) ask someone about their travel plans and describe your own travel plans,

( ) express a sequence of actions or events.

Name: ________________ Date: ____________

Lesson 19 Health and Medicine
第十九课 健康和医药

I. Listening Exercises

19-1 Listen to the dialogue between 黄飞 and 白雪. Then choose whether the following statements are true or false.

1. 白雪来美国三个月了。 True False
2. 白雪刚*来美国的时候喜欢吃美国菜。 True False
3. 白雪生病以后去看医生了。 True False
4. 白雪现在没有生病了。 True False
5. 白雪现在不喜欢吃美国菜了。 True False
6. 白雪现在还不会做美国菜。 True False

**Note:* 刚 [gāng]: just, recently

19-2 Listen to the dialogue. Then choose the best answer for each of the following questions.

1. Where are they going?
   a. They are going to her place.
   b. They are going to his dorm.
   c. They are going to school.
   d. They are going to the library.
2. How was she originally planning to go?
   a. She was going to ride her bicycle.
   b. She was going to take a bus.
   c. She was going to get a ride with someone.
   d. She was going to walk.
3. When did he buy his car?
   a. Today. b. Yesterday. c. Last week. d. Last month.
4. How long does it take to go to school by bus?
   a. An hour. b. Half an hour. c. Ten minutes. d. Five minutes.

19-3 Listen to the challenge dialogue. Though there may be some words and phrases that are unfamiliar to you, see if you can understand the general meaning by using what you have learned. Then choose whether the following statements are true or false.

1. They will go to see the doctor together.	True	False
2. He has a bad stomach ache.	True	False
3. She gave him some medicine.	True	False

19-4 Listen to the challenge dialogue again and choose the best answer for each of the following questions.

1. What is the time?

   a. 6:00 A.M. b. 7:00 A.M. c. 7:30 A.M. d. 8:00 A.M.

2. What is the relationship between the two people?

   a. Roommates.

   b. Friends.

   c. Boyfriend and girlfriend.

   d. Mother and son.

3. Will he go to see the doctor today?

   a. Yes. He will go after he gets up.

   b. Yes. He will go after he finishes his test.

   c. No. He cannot go because he has a test today.

   d. No. He will just take some over-the-counter medicine.

Name: ________________ Date: ____________

II. Character Exercises

19-5 Write the Chinese characters for the following Pinyin.

1. hǎoxiàng ____________
2. gǎnmào ____________
3. bǐjì ____________
4. fùxí ____________
5. shūfu ____________
6. zhǔnbèi ____________
7. gǎnxiè ____________
8. kǎoshì ____________
9. suǒyǐ ____________
10. yīshēng ____________
11. chīyào ____________
12. fāshāo ____________

19-6 Choose the correct traditional form for each of the following characters.

	a.	b.	c.
1. 头	a. 視	b. 開	c. 頭
2. 发	a. 條	b. 雙	c. 發
3. 药	a. 樣	b. 藥	c. 樂
4. 笔	a. 業	b. 醫	c. 筆
5. 备	a. 備	b. 準	c. 電
6. 医	a. 網	b. 醫	c. 習
7. 饿	a. 餓	b. 館	c. 飯

III. Grammar Exercises

19-7 For the following sentences, first change the sentence into a question. Then give a negative answer to the question.

1. 这个夏天我就要去北京学中文了。

Question: ____________________

Negative answer: ____________________

2. 她做了两个蛋糕。

Question: ____________________

Negative answer: ____________________

3. 我下了课以后，就去图书馆看书。

Question: ____________________

Negative answer: ____________________

4. 昨天我在我朋友家喝了很多酒。

Question: ____________________

Negative answer: ____________________

19-8 Unscramble the following sentences by placing the characters in the correct order.

1. 我/还/吃饭/呢/没有

 ____

2. 你/没有/了/吃药

 ____

3. 我/看/去/医生/了

 ____

4. 你/在家/应该/休息/地/好好

 ____

5. 我/考试/准备/地/好好/得

 ____

IV. Comprehensive Exercises

19-9 Translate the following sentences into Chinese.

1. I bought that red skirt tonight.

 ____

2. Let's go swimming together after you recover from your illness.

 ____

3. I haven't eaten at all today, so I feel very hungry now.

 ____

4. He has read three Chinese books.

 ____

5. I traveled to the West during spring break.

 ____

19-10 You have been staying up very late for several days and have caught a cold. You feel too sick to attend Chinese class today and plan to write a note to your teacher, which your classmate will take to class for you. Use the form below to write the note. (Use at least 80 characters.)

_____ 老师：

____

____

____

____

____

____

____

____

学生：(你的名字)

(　　年　　月　　日)

Progress Checklist

After this lesson, you should be able to use Chinese to:

(　) ask others if they are feeling well,

(　) ask others how they got sick and what symptoms they have,

(　) ask others if they have seen a doctor and if they are taking medicine,

(　) tell someone how you got sick and what symptoms you have,

(　) tell someone whether you've seen a doctor and what medicines you've taken,

(　) ask others if they have done a certain action yet and tell others if you have done something yet,

(　) indicate that a situation has changed.

Name: ____________________ Date: ______________

Lesson 20 Renting an Apartment
第二十课 看房和租房

I. Listening Exercises

20-1 Listen and choose the correct English meaning for each statement you hear.

1. a. I want to move in.
   b. I want to move out.
   c. I want you to move in.
   d. I want you to move out.

2. a. I brought my girlfriend over.
   b. I went out with my girlfriend.
   c. I went to see my girlfriend.
   d. I moved in with my girlfriend.

3. a. The rent has to be paid on the first day each month.
   b. The rent has to be paid in the first month every year.
   c. The rent has to be paid at the end of each month.
   d. The rent has to be paid on the first Monday of each month.

4. a. Please come over here right now.
   b. Please leave now.
   c. Please move in now.
   d. Please come down right now.

20-2 Listen to the dialogue between 小明 and 小谢. Then choose whether the following statements are true or false.

1. 那是小明的公寓，他们先在外面，然后进去。 True False
2. 那是小明的电视，他从家里搬过来的。 True False
3. 小谢把房租带来了。 True False
4. 房东太太*住在楼上。 True False
5. 小明上楼去把中文书给房东太太。 True False

**Note:* 房东太太 [fángdōng tàitai]: landlady

20-3 Listen to the challenge dialogue. Though there may be some words and phrases that are unfamiliar to you, see if you can understand the general meaning by using what you have learned. Then choose whether the following statements are true or false.

1. He wants to find a place close to where he works. True False
2. The place is close to a park. True False
3. The conversation is between a boss and an employee. True False

20-4 Listen to the challenge dialogue again and choose the best answer for each of the following questions.

1. What kind of place is he looking for?
   a. A two-bedroom apartment.
   b. A dorm room on campus.
   c. A place close to the park.
   d. An apartment close to campus.
2. Where does he work?
   a. In a university.
   b. In a park.
   c. At a real-estate company.
   d. At a telephone company.
3. How much is the monthly rent?
   a. $300 b. $400 c. $500 d. $540
4. When can he move in?
   a. Next week. b. In two days. c. Anytime. d. Next month.

Name: ________________ Date: ____________

II. Character Exercises

20-5 Write the following Pinyin sentences in Chinese characters.

1. Wǒ bǎ wǒ péngyou dàilái le.

____

2. Yǒu yíge rén bān chūqù le.

____

3. Nǐ yàobuyào bān jìnlái?

____

4. Qǐng nǐ bāng wǒ bǎ zhuōzi bān shàngqu.

____

5. Wǒ bǎ wǒde gǒu gěi wǒ nǚpéngyou le.

____

6. Wǒ mǎshàng xiàqu.

____

20-6 Match each traditional character with its simplified form.

_____	1. 須	a. 过
_____	2. 過	b. 马
_____	3. 樓	c. 须
_____	4. 來	d. 饭
_____	5. 馬	e. 来
_____	6. 進	f. 楼
_____	7. 飯	g. 进

III. Grammar Exercises

20-7 明学's Mom is coming to visit him the day after tomorrow. Use 把 and a directional complement to fill in the blanks in their phone conversation below. (Clues are given in parentheses.)

1. 明学：喂，是妈妈吗？我是明学。你后天 _____ 我的车 _____ _____ _____ 的时候 (when you drive my car over)，也 _____ 我的电脑 _____ _____ _____ (move my computer over)，好吗？

2. 妈妈：可以，要不要也 _____ 你的夏天衣服 _____ _____ _____ (bring your summer clothes over) 呢？

3. 明学：也好，一定要 _____ 那件黄衬衫 _____ _____ _____ (bring it over)，我很喜欢那件。

4. 妈妈：没问题。噢！对了，爸爸给你买了一个新手机。

   明学：太好了！请 _____ 那个新手机也 _____ _____ _____ (bring it over) 给我吧！

5. 妈妈：我今天做了饺子，要不要也 _____ 一些 _____ _____ (bring some over) 呢？

6. 明学：太好了，我的室友要 _____ _____ _____ 了 (move out)，他很喜欢吃饺子，你多拿一些 _____ _____ (take some over) 请他吃。

7. 妈妈：那我就多 _____ 一些 _____ _____ (take some over)。

明学：妈，我很累！我想再回 _____ (go back) 睡觉。

8. 妈妈：你昨天晚上是什么时候从学校回 _____ (go back) 的？

明学：我没有车，我是 _____ _____ _____ 的 (walk back)，十一点半才 _____ _____ (come back)。再见！

20-8 Answer the following questions about the dialogue above, using 把 and directional complements.

1. 明学的妈妈什么时候过去看他？

____

2. 妈妈要带什么过去？

____

3. 明学要妈妈把黄衬衫怎么样？

____

4. 新手机是谁买的？要怎么处理*呢？

____

5. 明学昨天晚上是什么时候回去的？

____

**Note:* 处理 [chǔlǐ]: deal with

IV. Comprehensive Exercises

20-9 Use 把 and directional complements to write a story about 一只小狗的生活 (a puppy's life). Try to write at least 8 sentences.

1. 

2. 

3. 

4. 

5. 

6. 

7. 

8. 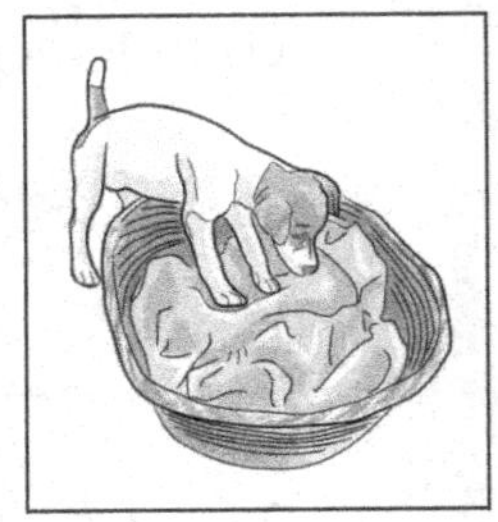

Progress Checklist

After this lesson, you should be able to use Chinese to:

( ) describe the direction of a movement or action,

( ) ask and answer questions about an apartment (such as what rooms are in the apartment, what is allowed, and when the rent is due),

( ) ask to go and see an apartment,

( ) ask someone whether they want to come over.

Name: ____________________ Date: ______________

Lesson 21 Future Plans
第二十一课 未来计划

I. Listening Exercises

21-1 Listen to the questions. Then write your answers in Chinese characters.

1. ______________________________

2. ______________________________

3. ______________________________

4. ______________________________

21-2 Listen to the challenge dialogue. Though there may be some words and phrases that are unfamiliar to you, see if you can understand the general meaning by using what you have learned. Then choose whether the following statements are true or false.

1. He will travel with some friends this summer. True False

2. She will do a summer internship with a company in Beijing. True False

3. She will visit her friends in China. True False

21-3 Listen to the challenge dialogue again and choose the best answer for each of the following questions.

1. Where will she go this summer?
   a. Mexico.
   b. Europe.
   c. China.
   d. Home.

2. When will she leave?
   a. Tomorrow.
   b. Next month.
   c. Next Monday.
   d. In two days.

3. What will he do this summer?
   a. He will go home.
   b. He will take some classes then go to the South.
   c. He will stay here.
   d. He will go to China.

II. Character Exercises

21-4 Use the given character to write a word or phrase that uses the same character.

Example: 校 学校

1. 意 ____________
2. 愉 ____________
3. 平 ____________
4. 运 ____________
5. 实 ____________
6. 假 ____________
7. 定 ____________
8. 留 ____________
9. 打 ____________
10. 申 ____________

Name: ____________ Date: ____________

21-5 Match the Chinese characters with the corresponding Pinyin.

_____	1. 找	a. kě
_____	2. 暑	b. zhǎo
_____	3. 研	c. diàn
_____	4. 可	d. bān
_____	5. 电	e. shǔ
_____	6. 班	f. jué
_____	7. 业	g. yán
_____	8. 决	h. yè

III. Grammar Exercises

21-6 What activities do you often do or like to do at the same time? Write six sentences using (一面……一面……/一边……一边……) to express things you often do at the same time or things that you like to do at the same time.

____

____

____

____

____

____

21-7 Choose the correct Chinese translation for each question or statement below.

1. Are you going to China soon?
   a. 你去中国了吗？
   b. 你去中国了没有？
   c. 你就要去中国了吗？

2. Have you taken the exam?
   a. 你参加考试了呢？
   b. 你参加考试了吗？
   c. 你开始考试了吗？

3. He is drinking coffee.
   a. 他喝了咖啡。
   b. 他喝咖啡了没有。
   c. 他正在喝咖啡呢。

4. I haven't gone to see doctor yet.
   a. 我还没有去看医生呢。
   b. 我去看了医生。
   c. 我就要去看医生了。

Name: ____________________ Date: ______________

IV. Comprehensive Exercises

21-8 What are your plans for this summer? What are your plans following graduation? Use at least 6 items from the box below and write a paragraph describing your plans for either this summer or after graduation. Try to write at least 15 sentences.

一面……一面……/一边……一边……				了	不……了	
就要……了	正在……	然后	以前	以后		
得	想	要	会	应该	觉得	把

____

____

____

____

____

____

____

____

____

____

____

____

Progress Checklist

After this lesson, you should be able to use Chinese to:

( ) ask someone what they want to do after graduation or in the summer,

( ) tell someone what you want to do after graduation or in the summer,

( ) ask someone when they will graduate,

( ) tell someone when you will graduate,

( ) ask someone when they plan to leave for a trip or tell someone when you plan to leave,

( ) describe actions being performed at the same time,

( ) wish people good luck when going on a trip or starting a new job.

Name: ____________________ Date: ______________

Lesson 22 Arts and Culture
第二十二课 艺术和文化

I. Listening Exercises

22-1 Listen to the passage. Then choose the best answer for each of the following questions.

1. How long has he been in Shanghai?
   a. A week.
   b. Four weeks.
   c. Two months.
   d. Four months.

2. When does class start every day?
   a. 7:30 A.M.
   b. 8:00 A.M.
   c. 8:30 A.M.
   d. 9:00 A.M.

3. What does he do every Wednesday morning?
   a. Takes Chinese class.
   b. Works in an American company.
   c. Goes to a friend's house.
   d. Visits some places in Shanghai.

4. What will he do next week?
   a. He will go sightseeing with friends.
   b. He will go out to eat with friends.
   c. He will intern at a company.
   d. He will learn how to drive in Shanghai.

22-2 Listen to the challenge dialogue. Though there may be some words and phrases that are unfamiliar to you, see if you can understand the general meaning by using what you have learned. Then choose whether the following statements are true or false.

1. She has had lots of homework recently.	True	False
2. He tried to find good food, but didn't have much luck.	True	False
3. She is looking for a new apartment.	True	False

22-3 Listen to the challenge dialogue again and choose the best answer for each of the following questions.

1. Where is he now?
   a. At home.
   b. In the South.
   c. In Europe.
   d. In China.

2. How long has he been there?
   a. Two days.
   b. Two weeks.
   c. A month.
   d. Two months.

3. When will he come back?
   a. Next month.
   b. Next week.
   c. In three days.
   d. Next Tuesday.

Name: ________________ Date: ____________

II. Character Exercises

22-4 Look at this lesson's Language in Use reading again. Find five words in the reading for each of the following categories and write down the characters next to each category.

1. People or things ______________________________
2. Action ______________________________
3. Time words ______________________________
4. Descriptive expressions ______________________________

22-5 Choose the correct traditional form for each of the following characters.

1. 丽 a. 讓 b. 廳 c. 麗
2. 剧 a. 劇 b. 時 c. 機
3. 东 a. 個 b. 東 c. 樂
4. 笼 a. 籃 b. 籠 c. 筆
5. 尝 a. 嚐 b. 聽 c. 電
6. 兴 a. 學 b. 興 c. 識
7. 处 a. 極 b. 運 c. 處

III. Grammar Exercises

22-6 Rewrite the following sentences using 因为……所以…… to give a reason for the event mentioned in the sentences.

Example: 我的中文进步得很快。

因为我常复习，所以我的中文进步得很快。

1. 我没去上课。 ______________________________
2. 我很喜欢这里。 ______________________________
3. 我没有给你打电话。 ______________________________
4. 我今天才给你写信。 ______________________________
5. 我今天起床起得很早。 ______________________________

22-7 Answer the questions below, using 比如 to give examples.

1. Which classes do you like?

____

2. What places would you like to travel to?

____

3. What kinds of food do you like to eat?

____

Name: ____________ Date: ____________

IV. Comprehensive Exercises

22-8 You are now studying Chinese in a summer program in Beijing. You have a room of your own at the dorm for foreign students. This is the third day after your arrival there. You are writing an email to your parents about your life and studies there. Because this is the first time you have traveled abroad, your parents are very concerned about you. Therefore, you should try to provide as many details as possible in your email!

爸爸、妈妈：

我到北京已经三天了。我在这儿都很好，我住在……

Progress Checklist

After this lesson, you should be able to use Chinese to:

( ) describe your current situation and ask others about what they have been doing lately,

( ) give examples,

( ) describe causes and effects,

( ) ask someone to write to you often,

( ) send your regards and wish someone well.